The Emotional Fire

The Fire That Burns Within

By Cynthia Powell

The Emotional Fire

The Fire That Burns Within

Copyright © 2015 by Cynthia Powell.

All rights reserved. No part of this publication may be reproduced, distributed or transmitted in any form or by any means, including photocopying, recording, or other electronic or mechanical methods, without the prior written permission of the publisher, except in the case of brief quotations embodied in critical reviews and certain other noncommercial uses permitted by copyright law.

The Emotional Fire / Cynthia Powell. -- 1st ed.
ISBN 978-0-692-93596-5

Dedication

I would like to dedicate *The Emotional Fire* to those of you who struggle to get out of bed every day trying to figure out where you fit in. To those who think they are not good enough, but you do not realize just how special you are Also, what matters is how you feel about you and not how other people perceive you. Remember to love yourself and forgive yourself because you are fearfully and wonderfully made!

I would like to send special love and a thank you to Pastor Gloria Taylor Boyce for her guidance and inspiration I would also like to send love out to those of you who have continued to love and support me

*Your current situation
does not define your destiny!*

Cynthia Powell

Forward

In Cynthia Powell's book *The Emotional Fire*, Cynthia uses her life experiences of how she overcame her troublesome past and put forward some guidelines that were helpful to her in that endeavor. In her works author Cynthia Powell talks about the importance of avoiding brooding over past hurts. The memories that you replay in your head only intensify and make you angrier. She said and I quote: "I felt the fire of life consume me. It felt like it was spreading and getting bigger". It does not mean you must cave in or give in to it. The journey may not be easy. You must keep it moving.

The theme behind this book is finding the way to restore our lost vision due to damage done to us as children. Another principle outlined by author Cynthia Powell was the importance of letting go of rejection. It is important for a child to comprehend how a trusted adult can hurt them that way. These deep hurts do not go away because you are now an adult. That feeling of rejection toys with your mind and is so distressing that it interferes with your ability to think and make decisions. Emotional scars and traumas can and will adversely affect your health and quality of life. For this reason, author Cynthia Powell, demonstrates in her book *The Emotional Fire,* just how to let go of that painful feeling of rejection. She said the sooner you let go of those painful rejections the better off your mental health will be. As I leave you with a segment taken from her book I want to strongly encourage you to obtain a copy of this book for every member of your family.

"Never be ashamed of your journey because it will help to inspire others. No matter what has happened in your life, know you have the strength. You can't change what happened physically and emotionally, but you have the power to come back from it. Your past has no power over your present. You are so much stronger than you give yourself credit for! It's something that happened to me but it is not who I am."

Pastor Gloria Taylor Boyce

Table of Contents

Dedication	i
Forward	iii
CHAPTER 1	**1**
The Fire of Life Consumed Me	1
Life Journey	4
We Had No Clue	8
CHAPTER 2	**11**
I Was an Absolute Hot Mess!	11
Marry or Not That Is The Question?	15
CHAPTER 3	**23**
The Things I Have Endured	23
Never in A Million Years	27
Everything Was Moving So Fast	29
On the Road to Recovery	31
CHAPTER 4	**33**
Trying To Make It Work	33
Enough was Enough	37
Learning Myself Again	39
Turning Fear into Confidence	41
CHAPTER 5	**45**
Hoping Things Will Turn Around	45
Excess Baggage	47
Kids Can Be So Cruel	50
CHAPTER 6	**57**
This Struggle Was Real	57
How Do I Heal	61
Rollercoaster Ride	64
CHAPTER 7	**67**
This Facility Was Interesting	67
Remember, Your Current Situation Does Not Define Your Destiny!	78
Glossary of Terms	81

CHAPTER 1

The Fire of Life Consumed Me

I felt the fire of life consume me. It felt like it was spreading and getting bigger but it doesn't mean you must cave in or give in. The journey may not be an easy one. You must keep it moving!

I went from grade school to junior high, for sure a different world. I was now going to school with older kids. They came from different areas and there were all kinds of personalities. It was interesting I will give it that! I understood how isolated I was after getting in school with other kids. Some of them were so hateful! Just imagine you come from a home where you were protected and loved to an environment of children from all walks of life. I was scared. I was unsure. High school was so different from grade school. I still felt like I was in grade school coming into high school as a freshman with all the older kids around. I wanted to be hopeful and optimistic about my future. I wanted to make some new friends. I tried to find my niche; with each day there was a new challenge. I wondered if I was up for the task. I was going to

The Emotional Fire

give it a try and see what happened. I was trying to put my best foot forward but it wasn't easy. I was getting adjusted to my new teachers and going from being in one classroom all day to now going to a different room for every class. It was quite the adventure! I was excited and nervous all at once. I was hoping I would get along with my new schoolmates. I was also smart enough to know to recognize I was a bit fluffier than the rest of the kids I encountered. Kids could be so mean and thoughtless! They called you all the typical fat nicknames you could possibly imagine but I pushed through it anyway because it wasn't like I could miss school because they were calling me names.

I really was hoping to be able to make new friends. I tried to get myself involved in activities in school so I wouldn't concentrate so much on my weight. Like that would really happen being a young lady and all; of course it bothered me. I started noticing boys on top of all these other crazy emotions. I even worried about the way I was dressed and that my clothes were just as together as the rest of my classmates. On top of all that, I started paying attention to knucklehead boys--just a problem waiting to happen.

It was my teenage hormones. Wouldn't you know it? Out of all the young men walking the hallway, I spotted this handsome guy; I found out his name was Leonardo. I never heard a name like that before. It wasn't a common one. I noticed him but he was not paying attention to me; at least, not at the beginning. He hadn't been in school for very long and he had a

Cynthia Powell

girlfriend already! Wow he worked fast but I wasn't surprised. I tried to stay out of his way since he didn't show any interest in me anyway. We just passed one another in the hall daily. He would talk to me sometimes at some of after-school functions. It truly was a one-sided crush on my part, since he had a girlfriend already. This went on for the rest of the school year. Before I knew the school year had zipped by. Summer was upon us but I didn't really do too much. I probably should have tried to get involved in some sports or something, but I just stayed around home. I would go outside to play every now and then.

Something I experienced at that time was having my yard TP'd as they called it back then (which meant toilet papering). Wikipedia's definition of toilet papering is 'the act of covering an object, such as a tree, house. Toilet papering can be an initiation, a joke, a prank, or an act of revenge.' I would have to clean up from this on a few occasions as a teenager. I remember this occurring when we first moved into the neighborhood. We were the first black family to move in an all-white neighborhood. It was for sure an interesting life experience. Our family moving in this area is what caused the toilet papering. So how do you live with or comprehend this happening when your parents didn't raise you to treat people differently no matter their ethnicity, race, social or religious group etc. it made for a compelling chain of events.

The Emotional Fire

The summer came and went, and school was back in session, with a new set of kids and new adventures to go along with it.

Life Journey

During my time attending school I had to go through being dark skinned and people thinking I wasn't smart and that I couldn't hold a conversation... Really! Go figure?!

How did they come to that perception because of skin color? From being called darkie to saying things like, "You're pretty for a dark-skinned person." To me when someone says that about a darker person's skin color they automatically think you're ugly. These *subtle* (read hurtful) comments can mess with your self-esteem. Can you see how all this being stuck in your head all through your life can cause future problems with your self-image into adulthood? I can remember as a child having white dolls with good hair. They don't look anything like me. I can recall getting my first chocolate doll. I was so excited. I never wanted another doll that didn't look like me again! The magazine even had the light-skinned sisters with good hair on the front of them. The skin bleaching thing was all the rage also. I even tried that dumb ass stuff too because I was lost. The toxic creams were stripping the melanin in my skin. How confused could I and so many others of us be as well? We needed to learn to embrace that we are more than our skin color even though at times it wasn't an easy task to overcome.

I must revert back to slavery when the dark slaves had to work in the fields and the light skinned slaves got to work in the master's house. Still today color plays a role in the definition of the concept of what beauty is. What a person becomes should be what they are judged on not the color of their skin. No disrespect to my light skin sisters, I love you all. I am just giving you my journey as a chocolate girl. Now I embrace my color, but I didn't always. Now I understand my truth much better! Understand me, I had no problem with my blackness, you know how cruel your peers can be and they can make you feel insignificant.

Here I was a fluffy girl and dark skinned, so at times it did mess with me. In different countries in the world, skin color played a part in what was considered beautiful. Light skin was a preference over dark skin. This affected Black Americans self-hatred toward one another. As part of our culture, it came from years of being oppressed and the hate inflicted by the slave owners The media was no help with this at all. They would portray dark skinned people negatively in the news, while light skinned and other non-black races were shown in a more positive light. So, growing up as child, where you're made fun of because of the color of your skin too was not much fun either. It could wreak havoc on your self-esteem for sure!

I was still trying to figure out who I was at this point. My hormones were all over the place.

The Emotional Fire

I didn't understand any of it. I was trying to get comfortable with my own self and my body. What a nightmare! It didn't stop my raging hormones from being on ten, so intense. I started noticing boys even though some of them were such jerks or was it their way of beating their chest to impress you, like a caveman (ha, ha, how lame. That didn't stop my eyes from roaming anyway. I really wasn't myself. It was those all-over-the-place, had me bouncing-off-the-wall hormones.

Now that we were back in school there were different classes and different teachers. Wouldn't you know it; I ended up having a class with Leonardo. I started trying to have conversations with him. He would to talk to me about the classes he was in and he asked me about some of the classes I liked too. At least he was talking to me, that was a start anyway! I will take it HA! HA! I know you're thinking: my parents didn't send me to school to think about big head boys. Like I said, them doggone hormones were something else gees!!! I did well academically and I was in the orchestra also. Leonardo started flirting with me. He would smile and wink at me sometimes and I would smile and wink right back! OH, MY GOODNESS! I was thinking with all that going on he was interested in me. I guess he was as interested as he could be at fourteen. He would ask me how I was and how my day was going, you know things like that. He seemed like he was a nice young man. I thought at this point I would ask if we could exchange phone numbers and talk sometime. The worse thing that could happen would be he'd say no and hurt my feelings. He ended up taking my number so I figured if he called me at least I'd know he was interested. I was hoping he'd call. About two weeks went by and he finally called. I was happy he called. We got a chance to find out what we had in common. We seemed to be getting along well, as things progressed. I'd say eight weeks or more went by, and we were talking regularly-- not sure if this was good or not. I felt like he considered me a friend. I had feelings for him, but we were on a friendship basis. Even though we had some intense conversations, as intense as they could have been at fourteen, 'em damned teenage hormones! I was not sure where this was going yet on his behalf. I probably shouldn't have been thinking about this at all but I guess I didn't have much control over my emotions then. He did mention that he cared about me. Maybe it was just agape love and I took it for more.

We were talking now on a regular basis since we were in a class together and we got to interact more in class now. He surprised me one day out of the blue and asked me if I would go out with him. I ask him what his girlfriend would think about that. He assured me that they were broken up. You know how boys can be; their hormones can be off the chain too! So maybe I should have found out what happened instead of going into it blindly; but I didn't, heaven help me. I said yes! For goodness sake, I was so naïve. We started dating--at least as close as you could get to going out on a date at our age (going to the library, doing homework and hanging out at afterschool functions). I was still too immature to be going on dates anyway.

There they go again those in my own world teenage hormone thoughts. I guess because this journey could be so random and have you all over the place.

We Had No Clue

It seemed to be going alright though as far as I knew even if I had nothing I could compare it to! In all young relationships, as we know, there are going to be some arguments. What did we know about it anyway! This is especially true when you try to act grown-up when you're not. We had no clue at all!

I didn't get my parents' permission to date because I knew they would say no, and that we were too young for that. I bet you guessed I did it anyway! The fact is I was so headstrong and didn't listen to my parents should have let me know it was not doing the right thing. It was still a learning process and we were still trying to understand our bodies and emotions. What really impressed me about him was the fact that he seemed to genuinely like me for who I was. That was new and it really left an imprint on me. The way he would hold my hand and look into my eyes, I felt he was really showing me his true feelings. We were trying to do this boyfriend/girlfriend thing, I guess, as much as we could being teenagers and not knowing the first thing about being in a relationship.

Cynthia Powell

We started having some small disagreements and he would get upset quickly and that worried me a little. I wondered how someone that young could get so heated but I just ignored it at first because maybe it was something going on with him that had nothing to do with me. I did keep this episode in my mental Rolodex though. I would forgive him because he'd apologize for his behavior. I just tried to accept him for who he was, even when he wasn't quite himself. I guess I was such the romantic even though I was not grown enough to totally understand that yet at all. I wanted to believe in unconditional love. I had to understand that you're going to have some good and bad moments.

Starting out as a young woman, I did not like or care for boys at all. I just wanted to beat up on boys when they came near me because of the crazy stories I would hear. "Pay attention: they only want to sleep with you to get notches on their belt." I figured the longer I could keep them off me by beating them up, the better off I would be. You know, sometimes my friends and I would hang out around the older boys, for the most part they would be cool until they would try to come at us. The things they would say to us were so nasty it was way too much to take. I really tried to stay away from them--way out of my league. Sex seemed to be the only thing in their heads. I had to realize as a young person sometimes when we're not around our parents we do some silly things without thinking. The things we know we weren't raised to do. Why is it we must learn a hard lesson before we listen to

The Emotional Fire

our parents? The school year was ending and I was still a virgin I was trying my best to stay that way. Boys can be so mischievous so they are going to try you. Leonardo was trying to wear me down; I guess he thought telling me he loved me would work. I did not cave in then, although we were both young and our hormones had no idea what sex was all about. It was always up for discussion. I was trying not to let him wear me down! In my heart, I knew I was not ready for sex at all, but my had-no-control-over-hormones took over. I let my guard down against my better judgement. If I had only followed my first mind it never would have happened. I didn't listen. I realized after that my mind and body were not physically and mentally ready for this at all! It was the most God-awful pain!

CHAPTER 2

I Was an Absolute Hot Mess!

It was quick and awkward, and all I wanted to do was take off running! Thinking to myself what the hell was I doing? My body may have looked like a grown woman but it wasn't ready for those grown women things.

I was so smart I didn't know I was pregnant. It wasn't all that for the first time so I didn't think that would even happen. HA! HA! It is funny now that I look back on it but it was not funny then. I just thought I came down with a bad case of the flu. I missed my period and that is something that never happened before. I should have known something was wrong because it showed up like clockwork. I didn't give it much thought that it was a little late. I was so immature, what did I know? I started feeling sick and I was throwing up a lot and my stomach hurt badly. I finally told my mom I felt lousy and she made a doctor's appointment for me. I still had no idea what was going on with me. I was going to the doctor to have my first

The Emotional Fire

vaginal exam. Nothing could have been stranger. I felt so violated. Then I heard the dreaded words I didn't want to hear: I was pregnant. I felt like I was going to faint. I thought my mom would be the upset one but she was calmer than ever. It was a good thing because I was an absolute hot mess. I felt like crap. I felt I had disappointed my parents. I think this all went down because my emotions were all over the place and I didn't know if I was coming or going. I thought I knew everything. How could I know more than my parents when they experienced all these things already? Wow, how smart could I be? I had no idea of my worth. I thought, "My goodness, I am a baby having a baby--either it is going to make me grow up or lose my way." Either way I must make a choice. I chose to be the responsible person, even at my young age, to be someone's mom the best I could. I had to get back after my shocking doctor's appointment. I hadn't come to grips with being pregnant myself. During the time I was in school it was not the "in" thing to be pregnant at a young age. It was like you had the plague, so I had to keep it a secret.

I was not ready to endure the backlash and shame. I was still trying to take it all in. The only thing I could do was hide it because I was a healthy young lady. I was lucky I didn't go through much morning sickness or any major signs until I got close to the end of my pregnancy. I had to hold it together until it was time to give birth. I was so stressed out just trying not to have any of the emotional pregnancy symptoms and keep it a secret. What a job that was by itself. I knew I would eventually leave school before I started to show. I had to think of what I could come up with so no one would ask me why I had to leave. I had to come up with a reason for being gone from school. I came up with saying my blood pressure was up so I get out with little questions as possible. I would have to worry about what to say after I was home. I was off for a few weeks, and I started getting phone calls from people who shouldn't have had my number but somehow did. I figured nobody would miss me once I was gone. Oh, boy I guess I was wrong. I realized they were just trying to find out my business, that's all. I told who I thought were a few of my close friends. I found out later I was wrong about that too! Those were the main one's doing all the gossiping about me. I never understood why teenagers felt the need to hurt and embarrass one another. These formative years are hard enough on their own.

Despite everything else, our daughter was born. Leonardo still didn't get it right. He was supposed to be working on us being a family, but he just couldn't get it together. It was so stressful and we were both so young and still trying to find our own way. I was now responsible for this precious life but didn't have a handle over my own. What was I to do? It was definitely an emotional rollercoaster. Can you imagine just after turning fifteen I was someone's mom? I was trying to master this task of being a mom while I still needed direction and guidance myself. I was a little nervous trying to figure this motherhood stuff out. I tried my best to give it

The Emotional Fire

my all. Every day was a task, some days downright frustrating. I often wanted to throw in the towel. What helped me push forward was looking into my beautiful little daughter's innocent face.

Leonardo really wasn't ready at all! His mind may have wanted a family but his body was that of an emotional hormonal teenager. I wanted us to work out but he was confused and not very sure of the direction he wanted his life to go in. Our relationship went through so many changes off and on for four years after our daughter was born. During this time, he talked about going into the Air Force. He didn't really ask me what I thought or felt about it. I wasn't happy about it at all. I felt he should have stayed here and help me take care of our daughter. Against my better judgement he decided to go anyway! I suppose he thought if he could have some type of career in the Air Force he could better provide for the family. Maybe it would help him grow up somehow.

It was a sad time. I didn't want him to leave because I cared about him. He was leaving to go to boot camp. He couldn't write right away because he had to get through basic training. It took around six weeks. I don't know what he was going through in basic training. Then he started writing about us being a family a lot and that was a surprise. I just thought maybe he was just lonely and homesick. As time went on I would say maybe around six weeks. I really don't know what happened I didn't get the whole story. He was writing me to tell me he would be coming home soon. He also was saying he missed me and how hard boot camp was. Now I can't tell you what could have happened to cause this next bit of information from him. All I know is he would be coming home on an honorable discharge. We didn't really talk about it much. When he finally got back home, he came over and helped me with the baby. I loved that I was thinking maybe there was some hope for us after all. A girl could dream can't she! I suppose all that family bonding we did made him say the next words from his mouth. He talked to me about us being a happy family. He wanted to get married.

It sounded good but I wasn't sure if I was ready for that yet. It would make an honest young lady out of me. I wanted to give us a chance. Maybe somehow, I could get my life together. Despite all the crazy scenarios going on in my head about why I shouldn't. I said yes anyway. A few months later, we tied the knot. My parents weren't happy about this union at all. They thought we were not ready; we were too young for this.

Marry or Not That Is The Question?

Fast-forward to the wedding day. I don't know if it was wedding jitters or what, I became a little nervous and apprehensive. I guess it was cold feet or maybe a sign not to do it, I don't know which one. I felt so strange about it the entire time before the ceremony, but I did it anyhow. We had the wedding at the church that we go to. I was over an hour late for the

The Emotional Fire

ceremony. What a catastrophe! Even after all those signs--my mom and dad told me I was too young to get married; they talked to me so long about it I was late; and that should have been my sign not to do it.

I still felt like it was the right thing to do. I felt I needed to grow up after having a baby and get out on my own, living my own life. You know how we young people are sometimes. We think we know it all, and just want to grow up and get out of our parents' house. Too many darn rules. If I wouldn't have thought I knew it all, I would have listened to my parents.

So here I was, 19 and a new wife and a mother--OH LORD I was struggling with both. I had not fully come to grips with being a mother, now I was someone's wife. I guess I thought I knew it all. I think as young people we think we have all the answers and know the answers more than our parents. We feel like all they do is tell us what to do. We don't get that it is their parental duty to give us guidance and discipline. It causes us to rebel because we just don't get it. That is why we end up having conflict with our parents. I understand why my mom and dad were not too happy with me. I was a young wife and mother. I know this wasn't their plan for my life. It wasn't what I had in mind either.

I fought with myself constantly. I wondered if I was good enough. I was so ashamed and embarrassed of the decisions and the things I had done in my life. I was such a hopeless romantic I was looking at marriage through rose colored glasses. Thinking I was a princess who had found her prince... It turned it to not be so. You see, not long after the wedding, things really started to change. The man I was so into, that I had a beautiful daughter with, and had now married began abusing me. He started by breaking me down mentally then physically. I was a wreck and even more ashamed of myself. I never asked for any of this. I was so unsure and always second-guessing myself. I had no idea how to fix myself or my situation. Another situation in my life I couldn't fix.

I wanted my mom and dad to be so proud of me. I wanted to show them, after I got married, that I could hold things down and make it work. Yet another dream was crumbling. I was shattered. My heart truly needed healing and so did my soul.

I tried to keep my head up, but on the inside my heart was really breaking. There was nothing more difficult than trying to hold it together. But no matter how hard I tried, it was falling apart. My faith was at an all-time low. I knew God was there. He was always around. I was so busy concentrating on the dark parts I couldn't see the light. I wasn't listening to Him. The truth was I wasn't trying to hear or understand Him. I couldn't see the light at the end of the tunnel, even though I really needed God's help. I wasn't ready to receive it at all. I was under some serious spiritual attack and trying to fight to get my life back. I was so frustrated with myself.

You know how it is, going from being in your parents' house to living with your husband. I tried to do the best I could. Little did I know

The Emotional Fire

what I was going to be up against. I was attempting to be a good young wife. I just tried to treat him like I wanted to be treated. That is all I knew how to do. I had so much on my plate we were going into a marriage blind and with a new baby.

We thought we were really in love and that was going to be enough. Even though we had so much to learn I was going to give it my best whole-hearted try. Apparently, we had different ideas on what marriage was about. I noticed in certain situations he was starting to become a little controlling. I thought a marriage was a partnership. We lived in an apartment complex. There were some married couples and some singles in the complex. When I would get off work and I would be around home, I would talk to some of my neighbors in passing. Leonardo would get upset when I talked to the neighbors. I didn't understand, unless he thought that there was more to it when I talk to some of the male neighbors. I was not doing that at all!

He was always accusing me of talking to them. As if I cared to, it took all the energy I had just to deal with one, so that wasn't happening at all. He started saying such hateful things to me. He was insulting me at every turn. When I would get all dressed up to go out and I thought I looked real nice, he would tell me how unappealing I was. He would say stuff like, "Who would want to look at you anyway?" It quickly became very frustrating! I didn't understand where these things were coming from. I didn't deserve this by any means! Something more had to be going on. Certainly something was not quite right, things were changing with him and his mood quit fast and in a hurry! You know how you feel like something is not quite right but you can't put your finger on it? My feelings soon proved to be true. I found out some time later the people he was calling his *friends* were the wrong people to be hanging out with. He would come home after being with those people and he would act so different, and he would start stupid fights with me. I wasn't sure at if he was doing a lot of drinking or drugs or both. I could really feel that something was wrong. I knew whatever he was dabbling in nothing good could come of it. He had turned into a totally different person.

I figured out over a period because of his mood and his behavior, he was indeed using drugs. It was not easy discovering that he was using. His mood swings! His short temper! It was not good at all. I decided to send our daughter to her grandmother's (my mom), for a while. I wanted her to be safe. It was one more thing for me to endure, but I did not want this for her. I thought it was best. I would just have to go home to my mom's and visit my daughter until things calmed down. It was no place for a child.

I was praying he would get some sense about himself. He was totally treating me like crap. He would say he was sorry so many times, and tell me how much he loved me and that he would do better. I loved him, you know, and I wanted to give him another chance. It was getting very frustrating because he would only do well for a short time. Then he just turned right back around to his old ways. At this point, we started

The Emotional Fire

fighting all the time. It was exhausting. Here I was a newlywed, and everything was going up in smoke already! I had no honeymoon stage. I felt like a total loser. I was just starting out and my marriage was already a mess. I sure hated being in the marriage. What the hell was I supposed to do now?

I would hear repeatedly in my head the words of the older church mothers that I looked to for guidance whenever I would think about leaving. They would say, "Baby, you have to stay and work out your marriage." They forgot to tell me all the hell and emotional things I would go through and how it would affect me mentally long-term by staying.

Oh, my goodness it wasn't easy by any means. I guess I just tried to fake it till I could make it. I realized I had bitten off more than I could chew. This was my damn bed and I had to lie in it, I guess, and even though I said that I loved him, I had no idea what that was about. I thought this drama was just a rough spot in my marriage. Thank God for my parents and the fact that they loved me and cared about me. I realize some kids don't have that unconditional love from their parents. I was grateful for that even though I didn't act like it at times. I would have not made it without their guidance. I would not have been married at nineteen if I had listened to my parent's advice.

The older you get you realize everything your parents told you would happen ends up coming to pass. I guess being young we think our parents are so lame and not cool at all. I found out that was not true at all. They truly loved me and only had my best interest at heart. The road I was trying to go down thinking I was so grown, they had seen and experienced already. How could I think I knew more than my parents?

I wish I could've run away from my marriage and not looked back, and gone back home and start over. I didn't want to because I thought I would hear, "I told you so" and all that stuff. That was not what I wanted to hear at all. I needed things to change and work out for me somehow. I just really tried to pull my way through it, but what a bumpy ass ride it was.

I found myself on my knees and praying to God for help and favor. You know the lines to the gospel song; "He may not come when you want him, but he'll be there right on time!" I could relate to the song I've been in the storm too long! I had been through so much physical and mental abuse. I didn't know how much more I could possibly take. I had lost sight of me totally. I felt like I was about at the end of my rope. I was looking for hope and some kind of help! Then wouldn't you know it a friend of mine invited Leonardo and me to church during their week revival. Once we walked into the service, it was as though God was speaking to both our hearts. That night in the church service changed our lives. The revival lasted for a week, but after the revival was over, we started going back to church on a regular basis again like we used to! What an awesome blessing! Things were starting to turn around. Not long afterwards, Leonardo came to me and said he felt God had called him to the ministry. He went to the pastor to ask if he could

The Emotional Fire

preach from time to time to see if he was ready for this. He was not too bad at it. He did well, so he decided to let him give it a try. He began to preach more often. We were even getting along much better at home. That was a delightful change.

It was almost like we were newlyweds again. He made me remember what it was I loved about him in the first place. I started feeling like I could finally be happy again. We started doing more things together. It was really a nice change, we started going on weekend trips. We went out on romantic dinners and just enjoyed each other again!

You know he even took it upon himself one time to surprise me on our anniversary, and took me to a beautiful cabin-style hotel. It was like a honeymoon. We didn't have one when we first got married, but we were having one now and it was wonderful. I was praying with all my heart this would continue! Somehow, I had hoped our marriage would be a success.

To my dismay the loving streak didn't last. I noticed right away his old *friends* started coming back around. I knew they didn't mean him any good! I suppose he wasn't strong enough to resist the temptation like he thought.

CHAPTER 3

The Things I Have Endured

Would you believe the next six or seven years were unbelievable--the things I endured? They were not easy. I would just sometimes go to the church mothers since I was in church and ask their advice on marriage, especially when you had some problems. They would say "stay and work through it." The church would preach against divorce but some situations were unbearable! There was no way that was possible at times. With all the arguments and fights, it was worse than ever before. I never knew what would set him off, so I had to be really careful. He would get so upset and go off on me for no reason at all.

One time while we were arguing and he was talking to me, he caught me off guard and hit me square in my face. He struck me so hard that he dislocated my jaw. At that time, we had no insurance and I couldn't go to the doctor. To this day when the weather changes it bothers me. I have lived with this for so many years.

I could not begin to tell what I did or how to explain what happened during our conversation

The Emotional Fire

as to why he even did it. I quit asking him why. I don't think he even had a grip on why.

When it came to the intimate relations in our marriage, I would have to constantly fight him off. He started forcing himself on me. How could someone say they love you and do things like that to you? I don't know how, after all the abuse I had been through with him, he would think I would want to be bothered with him at all. He forced himself on me so much it got to the point that he would sodomize me again and again by force. He was always accusing me of cheating on him. Justifying his actions, I guess. I was so stressed out and confused all the time. I had no idea what to do. I couldn't tell anyone.

I was more worried about anyone finding out what the hell I was really going through. I was so embarrassed and worried that someone would tell me just how stupid I was for putting up with all this crap. I know people always say you could have found someone to talk to. "Yeah right," I had tried that many times before and it never worked out well for me. I wasn't strong enough yet at that time. My self-esteem was not in the best place at all. I felt that whoever I would talk to would judge me anyway. I would beat up on myself so much. I felt like I totally let my parents down, and my daughter as well as myself.

After all I had been through, would you believe I was pregnant again with our second child? It wasn't a happy pregnancy like it was supposed to be. I was stressed out to no end and crying all the time. It was so much at one time! I didn't take care of myself at all. He would start that same crap, talking down to me and accusing me of messing around on him. "Really? Seriously? You have got to be kidding me!"

I was pregnant. I was working all the time, and he was not working at all, at the time. As a matter of fact, I was working two jobs would you believe while I was pregnant! He was home all day, and did not help with cleaning or anything. It was so damned frustrating! He would leave everything for me to do when I got home.

Even though he was treating me like shit, I tried not to break his spirit when he still was not working and could not find a job. I only wish he knew how to keep me lifted as well. I would work until very late at night. I was exhausted. As hard as I was working to hold us together, the controlling behavior went from one extreme to the other. It was a darn rollercoaster ride. He wanted me to clean and then he didn't want me to clean. If I didn't clean up, he would use it to pick a fight with me the next morning.

We were arguing one time, and instead of us both getting bent out of shape and both getting heated, I decided to leave to give us both time to really cool off.

OH, MY GOODNESS as I walked down the stairs to leave, he decided to pick up the television and threw it down the stairs at me. It hit me and grazed me across my back. Why would he do that, I was pregnant at the time?! I was truly going through the worst kind of hell? I know you probably don't know why I am even still hanging in there. But like most impressionable young girls who have never experienced any other young men. He was my first love. He was my high school sweetheart. He was my first everything.

He begged me to forgive him and kept telling me he loved me. I think he just didn't want me to leave him. He asked me again to give him another chance to get his damned act together. I don't know if my body was just going through so many doggone changes and playing with my emotions, but I dared to give him yet another chance. I was on such a crazy emotional rollercoaster. Even as I forgave him, I was also disappointed in myself. I was pregnant again in this screwed up union I was in and had no idea how the hell to get out. I had so many thoughts going through my head, and none of them were sound choices. I was pregnant, and my emotions were all over the place, and I was not eating properly. My spirit was broken. I just kept pushing myself despite being an emotional mess. It was not an easy task at all.

I was still working hard to keep the family afloat. I was working in the kitchen and I would have to pick up heavy trays full of dishes to put in the dishwasher. But this one night at work, I went to pick up a tray of dishes and I got an awful pain in my stomach. It hurt so bad I had to go to the emergency room. They told me I had gone into early labor, and I had to stay at the hospital until the contractions totally stopped because it was too early for that. There was so much going on.

Cynthia Powell

Never in A Million Years

I knew things were getting even more difficult but I never would have imagined in a million years my day would end up with me looking in the barrel of a gun. I thought it was going to be a nice day with Leonardo just coming home from work and me cooking a nice dinner. Instead, I didn't know if he had a bad day or what, but nonetheless he walked into the house with an attitude and started an argument. I was in the kitchen just cleaning it up. We started out with a conversation that turned into harsh words. I don't even know how we got here. But we ended up arguing to the point he ended all up in my face. I was really scared. So, when he walks toward me aggressively, I had to pick up a knife and shake it at him to get him out of my face. I wasn't sure of what he was capable of. I had experienced some rough things with him in the past. He walked away and went into the bedroom and closed the door. After that I threw the knife back in the sink. There were so many thoughts going through my head I never could have imagined what was coming for me next!

Since we were in a full-blown fight, I decided to be the one to leave so it wouldn't escalate any further. I walked to the closet to put my coat on before leaving. Suddenly I heard the bedroom door fling open. He called out to me first, only for me to look at him pointing a gun at me from the bedroom. I was really shocked, and I just froze in my tracks. I asked him what in the world was he doing. He didn't respond. I guess he

The Emotional Fire

didn't hear me. Bang! I was shot. I couldn't believe it.

If he hadn't called out to me before he shot, I would not have moved my head, which was in front of the hand that was holding the closet door. The bullet would have gone right through my temple. Instead, when the gun fired, the bullet hit me in the hand--which was still holding on to the door. The bullet went into my hand but it didn't come out. It felt so strange, it stung and burned. It swelled up immediately! My hand was three times its size.

I couldn't move. I was in shock. I couldn't bring myself to believe my husband had shot me! I couldn't believe it'd come to this! It was horrible, there was so much blood. It was such a frightful scene. I think after the smoke cloud cleared, he saw me holding onto my hand and all the blood that was splattering, and I think he realized what he'd done. He was petrified.

I had never seen so much blood before. It was squirting out just like a water fountain. Leonardo wrapped my hand up and got me into the car. The whole ride to the hospital I was thinking, "He really shot me. I don't believe it." I am sure I was in shock. He was yet again apologizing and telling me how much he loved me. Yes, again. OH, MY GOODNESS!

It really freaked him out seeing so much blood. It made him nervous. I would have thought I would be all panicky and crazy, but to my amazement, I was calm. I'm sure my body was in total shock mode, and that was why. It was unbelievable that something like this could have happened. It is not something you would think of happening to you at all. It is a line you think will never be crossed.

Everything Was Moving So Fast

Now by this time I entered the emergency room, things began moving very fast. They took me right into the emergency room and prep me for surgery, for my gunshot wound. They told me it was a great possibility that I could lose my middle finger on my right hand. They were concerned about that happening. They weren't sure if they would be able to save it or not. I was in surgery for around eight hours. I was so grateful to the good Lord for working through the surgeons. They could save my finger after all. "Glory be to God!" I had to stay in the hospital about a week to recover.

But I found out later after coming out of surgery that the police had talked to Leonardo and he told them how it all happened. In fact, because he shot me, they immediately arrested him. He was in jail for a week. When he got out, he came straight home. I know I probably shouldn't have let him come back but damn it I did it anyway. He started telling me how sorry he was, like he had done so many times before, and he wanted our marriage to still have a chance, I guess. What really blew my mind after everything that happened was that they gave him back his gun but didn't give me back my kitchen knife! What kind of bull crap was that

The Emotional Fire

anyhow? It made no sense to me at all. It sent a clear message. Especially the way they handled this whole thing not well at all.

I know you are still wondering what the hell I was doing and thinking. I had so many things running through my head. I wasn't feeling good about myself, but I was thinking I believed that I loved him so much that my love would help save him. I had so many physical and emotional issues my own. I didn't know what was real and what wasn't at this point. I wanted to try to make it work. I wanted to prove to myself that I had some fight left in me and I wasn't a total failure. I didn't say I always think clearly or make the right choices.

I guess I felt at the time these were choices I made and I had to suffer through it. When someone tells you they love and how sorry they are for causing you pain, you really want to believe that they are telling the truth. Emotional madness, that's what I call it sometimes when you keep doing the same thing over expecting a very different result! I guess I just always tried to see the good in every situation. With the hope that someday it would change for the better. I just never knew what to expect.

Leonardo and I had been home together for a week after this ordeal. It was interesting I will give it that. I would think by now you'd think I had lost my ever-loving mind. What in God's name was I doing? My self-esteem wasn't good at all, not good enough to fight back yet. Sometimes your actions don't reflect your thoughts. Either I temporarily lost my mind or I had the biggest heart ever, despite the things I been through.

After being home with me for a while, it was tension-filled for sure. Leonardo's mind was starting to get the best of him. I was cooking for him like wives do, and he started accusing me of poisoning his food. I wasn't at all. His conscience was really getting the best of him. It wasn't a thought on my part at all, but he didn't trust me. Would you believe it? I think it should have been the other way around. For me, I needed to forgive him from my heart--that was the only way I could try to make it work. I didn't want two wrongs to make a right. If you can understand my point. I didn't understand his thought process, if he felt uneasy around me why did he continue to do annoying things?

On the Road to Recovery

I was on the road to recovery. I would soon be able to get back to work. I thought I would finally get a break from some of the emotional shenanigans. I worked next door to where we lived at the time. I would go to work the same time every day. On break, I would go home every now and then since I was so close. I went home once, only to find a woman in my house with my husband. Of course, he told me to just to get whatever it was I needed, not to say anything, and go back to work. I did just that! My first thought was "How stupid could I be?" I had to face the fact I wasn't strong enough yet, such an awful feeling. My next thought was I wanted to

The Emotional Fire

beat my husband's ass after all the craziness I had been through with him. I know that wouldn't have gone well because I couldn't win. I told myself that I was working and there was nothing I could do about it right at that moment. It was the longest and frustrating night ever. I was so hurt. I decided I would try to call him on my next break. What happened next I never saw coming! Would you believe that same woman who was there earlier had the nerve to answer the phone? I couldn't get over it! What the hell was really going on? Really!

I had finally worked my shift till it was over (longest night ever)! He was smug. I felt so hurt and betrayed. I had no idea what to do about it. My self-esteem was at an all-time low. I was so confused and I had no one I could even talk to, no one that I could really trust. I was worried if I told somebody about what I was going through, he or she would tell me I had lost my ever-loving mind. I felt like such a loser and failure.

CHAPTER 4

Trying To Make It Work

With all the things I had happen in my life, I wondered why I couldn't get it together. Why was I trying so hard to make it work? I had so many crazy thoughts going on in my head. I felt like I wasn't good enough nor that I even deserved to be happy. I had two daughters, that I loved more than life itself and I was trying to be a good mom to them. I was trying to do my best to hold my family together. My self-esteem was literally on the bottom of my shoe. I felt so bad. I could not see past my pain. What was I even teaching my babies? I never wanted my girls to see me hurting or going through some of the awful things in my life. But this was no life to have.

Everyone needs someone to talk to sometime or another. I thought I had really found that friend I could talk to. So, I decided to open up and share my experience.

Just when I thought I could finally trust someone again, she turned on me. That so-called

The Emotional Fire

best friend ended up telling other people all my personal business. I was devastated. I felt so betrayed and I didn't want to feel this way. My hope one day is that this inner pain would subside.

People were talking about me behind my back and smiling to my face or should I say laughing at me as well. Do you realize how hard it is to open up to anyone when someone has already betrayed you with your deepest darkest life shames? It caused me to shut down totally.

I just wanted to bury everything deep down inside. I kept it all in. It made me distance myself from people period! People can be so damned cruel, thoughtless, and totally unfeeling until it's all about them. I was emotionally damaged from physical and sexual abuse. I didn't know who I could talk to or who I could even trust. Some people treat you any way they want without any regard for your feelings that occurs from their actions. I didn't want anyone to go through the hurt and pain like I had. I worried constantly about what people thought about me. And on top of everything else, some people are just something else. Instead, of lifting you up and giving you some encouragement, they make it their mission to tear you down. I had never done anything to any of them, but they decided they didn't like me and therefore it was okay to cause me pain and anguish in my darkest hour. I could never understand how people could speak about you when they didn't even know you.

Cynthia Powell

Most people take your kindness for weakness. Then they wonder why you don't want to be bothered. They mistake being quiet for being withdrawn. I am so glad I still have a forgiving heart after all the foolery I've been through. I have room to love people and not react to them like they did me when really I shouldn't have given any of them chances at all.

You know, sometimes the things you go through in your life can cause you to make some very bad decisions if you don't think it through. I had regrets about some of them. No doubt about that. It wasn't easy. I was so disappointed, especially at myself. When it came to men, it was really beyond my understanding. I never seemed to pick the right one. I guess I didn't have any idea at this point what a right one was. I was looking for someone to love me and tell me I was the one as all young ladies do. I didn't realize so many of them were full of crap and they just tell you what you want to hear so they can sleep with you! Go figure.

It took me a while to understand that you should not take someone at their word. It got so bad I trusted no one at all. I went through so many different changes and emotions. I even got to the point that I didn't want to get dressed or get out of bed. I had been through a million changes and back again! I went from being angry to crying to feeling betrayed and used. I promised myself no matter how crappy people had treated me in my past my heart wouldn't let me stoop to the same level as they had. Even though I had my own struggles I didn't want to block my blessings. I know what it is like to be hurt and let down. It was the worst feeling ever.

I mustered the inner strength to know I wanted to give my family and my few good friends the love I never received. What came out of these experiences helped me learn how to be a good friend and love my family unconditionally. I know people can say and do hurtful things to you that can affect your whole being! I tried to live by the 'fake it till I become it' motto. I had to recall this when I needed to. It was such a lonely place to be. Because I was dealing with so much and having no one to trust to unload, the burden was devastating. I found myself so stressed out. It took so much energy to keep things under wraps.

Leonardo was supposed to be in the ministry as a preacher during this time, but he was not treating me well at all. Certainly, not like a preacher should be. However, I did not want to talk to a pastor considering I was married to a so-called one, not a good example at that time at all. I thought about talking to a therapist, but I figured I would just end up being a case study and maybe he and or she really couldn't or wouldn't help me at all.

But maybe as much as I disliked the fact, maybe I did need to talk to a professional. I thought maybe a therapist could at least help me sort out some of these stressful emotions I was going through. There came an opportunity for me to be able to talk to a counselor. I was so nervous about going to this appointment because it meant I had to open up. This was not easy for me at all. I have had a wall up for so long after so much heartache. I didn't know if I was coming or going. Once we started talking, I did open up and talked a little. I didn't open up completely because of past experiences with people violating my trust. I had to admit to myself that I did feel somewhat better after the conversation. But it made me feel so vulnerable. I went that one time only to see a counselor and have never been back since. In the end, I suppose that with the passing of time the heartache, disappointment and frustration would somehow self-repair and I would come out whole and victorious. That was my wish.

Enough was Enough

I finally, at some point, had to realize enough was enough. I had given it my all and had no more to give. I finally got my nerve up to leave Leonardo. It truly was a mental and emotional struggle for me to do it. I didn't look back, like I had so many times before. I finally left Decatur. I couldn't believe I finally had the courage to do it. My babies and I moved backed to Joliet. I had to try to start over, begin picking up the pieces of my damned screwed up life, and try to get it together.

I had no idea where I should begin. I was broken, and I needed to be fixed. I had to figure out how to start loving myself again, especially when I had no clue what that was about. My way of dealing with it at the time was just by staying in the house. That is all I knew how to do. I

The Emotional Fire

would stay away from interacting with people as much as I could. Because at this point I had to force myself to get dressed and get out of bed. I would use that 'fake it till I become it' motto. I wished myself good luck with that one! It was such a long and painful journey for me.

My self-esteem struggles were listening to some people tell me I had a pretty face but I needed to lose some weight. Such a not-so-nice, backhanded comment. But because I really understood how it felt to hear that, I was nice enough not mention other people's flaws and issues. I truly knew firsthand how it felt to be insulted to your face. I held back from giving them the same disrespect in return. I mean for real, do you think people who are overweight don't know this already? They do every day of their lives but people that don't have this issue truly don't understand. They certainly don't need anyone else to bring this to their attention.

If you don't understand the journey it is best to just shut up! You can be healthy, exercise and still be overweight in people's eyes. You can have a medical condition, or have been sexually molested and gain weight because of not being comfortable in your own skin. If you have no idea of what a person has been through, you really can't comment on it, nor should you speak on it. They have experienced enough of this already.

Here I was attempting to put together the shattered pieces of my life and I had no one I could trust or talk to at all about any of it. So, for me food became my comfort! The reason is that food doesn't talk back. It doesn't put you down, it doesn't judge you or call you names. It doesn't talk about behind your back either. It gives you the comfort you want.

I knew I had to change my way of thinking eventually. I was so much more comfortable with enjoying my food than talking to people. This is not what I really wanted for myself. It was not the normal I desired. I had to figure a way out.

Learning Myself Again

It was a task for me to start to learn about myself again. I wasn't sure if I really knew myself at all, I had to try to figure it out. I had to start somewhere. I decided to start figuring out the food I was consuming and maybe start to change some of that. It was a journey, you know? That was something that hopefully I could change and get some type of handle on it. So, I started where I had control. I cut some things, I began eating healthier, and doing some exercise. I had to talk to myself on a regular basis to stay on track.

I tried to work on my outside first, hoping it would fix the broken me inside at some point. I had to learn to love and care about me again. I had to understand that I was worth it and not totally worthless. I had to realize my importance on this earth. It was surely my true struggle.

It was so easy for me to fall back into old habits because when you're on a weight loss

The Emotional Fire

journey sometimes you must become your own darned cheerleader. Sometimes people don't want you to succeed. When they're not in a good place, people like you right where you are. That way they can define you against themselves. I realized I had to continually find the strength inside of me if I was to achieve my goals. I wanted so much more for my babies. I wanted to be the best mom I could be, a better woman for my girls. I always tell them they can do anything they put their minds to. I wanted to show them they could do it as well.

I would always let them know how beautiful and smart they are. I never wanted them to go through the things I had been through--not ever. I wanted to protect them from everything. Even though I knew in my heart of hearts it wasn't possible, but I damn sure was going to try my best. I didn't want to be such a disappointment to them. I wanted them to be proud of me.

Motherhood didn't come with a manual, so I had to learn by trial and error. Sometimes balancing everything is overwhelming. Even trying to do the logical and expected things, like keeping a roof over our heads and keep the bills paid, I hated. I knew I had to be responsible but it meant I had to sacrifice the time I could spend with my girls to provide the necessities. But that is part of motherhood, what are you going to do?

What I had to realize and get through to myself was that it didn't matter what anyone else thought about me. *It was what I thought about myself.* I had to build my own confidence in myself and do the best I could. There were times

I would feel uncomfortable because I would walk into rooms while people were having conversations and realized when I walked in the room, they were whispering about me. Not the best feeling at all! They would say I was lazy, unhealthy, and whatever else they could come up with. It was hard enough especially when you're dealing with your self-esteem issues. It was not true. I was working my butt off and carrying my own heavy life load. It reinforced my internalizing and self-cheerleading. I hadn't gotten to the place yet in my life to realize I wasn't the problem. It was not until later that I understood that the ones who were talking about me had to find flaws in me so they wouldn't have to concentrate on their own issues. Sooner or later, I found out they all had them. Despite all my efforts to try to move ahead, I needed some soul healing. I equated being silent with being strong. It only caused me to bury things even deeper.

Turning Fear into Confidence

Then, one day something happened. A memory entered my head and came up and out. And then I thought, "To get where you ought to be you have to remember where you came from." It's how you deal with your issues and come out on the other side that counts! I had to figure out how to turn my fear into total confidence.

I was very cautious and apprehensive around people. They could be so cruel and unfeeling at times. I had been stabbed in the

The Emotional Fire

back so many times there was nowhere else you could possibly stick me. So, I put myself out there to be stuck again and tested the waters with different people. I would tell them some half truths about me just to see were the chips would fall. It was so hard for me to trust so I had to try to work through it. Sure enough, it kept repeating itself: failure after failure. But when the smoke did clear and the information got back to me, there was much more to the story than before and none of it was true.

I got so tired of putting my heart out there and getting it crushed. It was hard to recover from each disappointment. I would keep putting my heart out there though. I kept trying to have a real, truthful and trusting relationship with someone. There is no way it could possibly get any worse. The only way I could go was up after all. That was truly my hope anyway! Starting over was a constant struggle. I knew somewhere, deep down inside I was worth it though. I still wasn't totally convinced after all the time that had passed, but I was still moving forward and the weight of yesterday never seemed to let up. It was so daunting.

I had been away from Leonardo for some time now, about eleven years. Even though I was still going on with my life, I was still legally married, we were just not living together anymore. I decided it was finally time for some closure, and took steps toward getting a divorce. While starting this process, I got a phone call letting me know Leonardo had gotten married again!

Cynthia Powell

I guess so much time had gone by, he thought we weren't still married. I told him guess again we are still legally married. I really didn't make a big deal about it. I was so glad to be away from him. I had somebody in the family tell him that his new wife wasn't legitimate at all. So I kept on moving forward with the divorce. I was so happy and excited when it was finally done and over with. It was like I could breathe again! It was a long, stressful process for sure. Divorce is never good; it's a breakdown of a family unit that was supposed to be forever. Despite feeling relieved, I was still on an emotional rollercoaster. It was like I lost a piece of myself. You feel like you somehow can never get that piece of yourself back again!

My divorce was finally done and over with. I had some mixed emotions and I was trying to work through it. I can't tell you that I wasn't a little scared, but I was relieved too. I had to come to the reality that it was over. Now, it was about me and my babies. I had to get on with my life and get normalcy back if that was possible. This one was all on me. I was officially a single mom. Oh my goodness, this was so scary to say out loud! It just gave me one more thing to feel inadequate about. Oh boy! It was just me and the girls. I had to try my best to see the light at the end of the tunnel for their sake, while at the same time trying to get my act together. It was so overwhelming at first. It came along with plenty of tears and some setbacks. I had to push my way through it, and try to keep my head up at the same time. I tried to keep up a good face for

The Emotional Fire

the girls not matter what, hoping it wouldn't affect them in any way.

There were so many rough days. I never wanted them to see me cry. I would wake up so many mornings not wanting to get out of bed, but I had to push through it for the girls. I had to try to give them a decent life somehow. I really had to work on building my faith. I was slowly getting stronger on my feet as I prayed constantly on my knees.

CHAPTER 5

Hoping Things Will Turn Around

Praise God, things seem to start turning around. I did finally get a job and could take better care of the girls. What an absolute blessing this was! It was a good start. I was playing catch-up with everything. But I was so grateful to finally be able to even do that. Even though I had a job, the pay wasn't very good. I had to make due during this time. I was always looking for a better job and something with health benefits for my girls. They had some asthma and ear infection issues. I was always in the emergency room with them, which caused a lot of bills. I had to do what I had to do. During this time, I was working a full-time job and two part-time jobs working thirty-five additional hours a piece per week just to survived.

I was living my life on my own terms and trying to do the best I could to make ends meet. I was trying to keep myself lifted and encouraged. I got a call that would change my comprehension. In June 2005, I got a call that

The Emotional Fire

Leonardo had brutally killed a young lady. I was in such terrible shock by this news! I realized at that very moment he had issues much deeper than my understanding, and more than I could love him through. I had gained some issues from being with him without a doubt! But I realized I could have not fixed him, no matter how much I thought I could. After hanging up the phone, with tears streaming down my face, I thanked the creator and was just grateful because that could have very well been me. What he needed was beyond my control. I think I was still in denial hearing the news but when I read the newspaper article that made it real me at this point.

I realized that everything that happened to me wasn't my fault and I could never have seen it coming. I really thought my love for him would somehow be able to save him. When I gave up on that idea, I totally ended up saving myself. So many things were going around and around in my head. I relived all the things he had done to me repeatedly. I just thought to myself at any time that could have been me. I might not have been around at all. So much was released from my spirit. Such clarity came to me even in the presence of this bad news. I thank the Lord for his favor, grace, and amazing mercy. I held on the thought that God truly protected me and that God really does not put more on us than we can bear. I understood at that moment, I was strong, I was deserving. My journey was just beginning; it was not over by a long shot. My struggle still not over.

Cynthia Powell

I was working three jobs so the girls and I would have a roof over our heads. I hated not being able to spend as much quality time as I wanted to with them. I had to sometimes go back and forth with myself. I had to take care of my financial responsibilities, and my girls were growing up before my very eyes! I truly was burning in an emotional fire, so many decisions to make not knowing which direction to go in! I really tried to be there for them as much as I could when they needed me. It was taking a toll on me mentally and physically. I really needed to find one good job with benefits. It was a constant struggle! I was always trying to keep my game face on!

Excess Baggage

In the meantime, the fire of emotion for me was I had to decide to put my excess baggage on hold so I could somehow keep it together for my daughters. I never felt okay when I had to leave Tiffini and Tamyka. I felt like I was failing as a mom. I kept pushing forward hoping things would get better for me. I came from so much emotional baggage just trying to unpack and sort it all out. I had to talk to myself on a regular basis. It was exhausting at times trying to always keep it together. I had some deep self-esteem issues. I always felt like I was not good enough.

I can remember when I was pregnant with our second child, Leonardo took me through so much drama. We had separated; I was living with my in-laws and I had no car so they would give me rides to work when they could otherwise I would walk to work. I was walking to work one day and Leonardo picked me up. He was such a butthead when it was time to let me out of the car. He would start moving the car when I would get out so I would literally have to jump out of the car while he was driving. I never thought he would do that or treat me like that. It devastated me that he felt that way about me to handle me and his unborn daughter in that way.

No matter the situations I was in when I conceived, the results were both of my beautiful daughters and I loved them very much. So, you see I really thought I had side-stepped a lot of things in my life but I still had not. I just replaced them with other things. There were some things I was not so proud of. I am sure everyone sometime or another has done things in their life they wished they could erase. The thing is though wither they were private things or public things that happened, they still affected my life deeply. I tried to remind myself that this was not my destiny but a life journey I was on! It did not define me. Thank goodness it did not!

I hadn't had any professional help while going through my life lessons. I was just trying to figure it out on my own. When I got pregnant at fifteen, I did not get pregnant to keep a boyfriend. I did not understand what a boyfriend really was. I only knew what I was told by my friends. It truly was a rude awakening! I didn't understand these emotions at all! If that wasn't enough I had a very hard outlook of my body image! I wasn't sure what was expected and what wasn't let alone all the other things I was

Cynthia Powell

going through as a young lady! It was a lot of pressure! Who wouldn't want to be popular or have a lot of friends and sometimes be the center of attention? Let's just be real! How could you have good feeling about your look after the women they show on ads and on TV? It would cause you to be very critical of yourself. Body image worries and eating disorders are very similar. As a matter, a fact not being happy with your appearance as a teenager can cause you to go on an extreme diet, take diet pills, and try all kinds of things to accomplish this. It could also lead to things like anorexia, bulimia, compulsive overeating and binge eating. It really causes so many issues trying to live up to all these expectations! The way we feel about our bodies plays an important role in our self-esteem. If we are so hard on ourselves about the way we look, we can start to feel inadequate, alienated and ashamed of our looks. Oh, my goodness, the pressure of this during school years is a lot of weight on your shoulders! I could only imagine and not understand from childhood to young adulthood the ups and downs that your body goes through just trying to cope with your emotions and coming to grips with figuring out who you really are! This can be a traumatic time in your life!

This is a real thing. Some don't understand this or those for whom it has never been their issue won't ever get it! When you have been so overly hard on yourself for a long time, it can put some major thoughts in your head that are hard to let go of. I really had to learn how to accept me on a regular basis. It took an ongoing talk with myself after the journey I had been on! I was bound and determined to change this no matter what, even though my attempt at it sometimes didn't work out; but I wasn't going to stop until I somehow could get it right. It took my life's voyage to all different levels!!

If you girls are trying to get pregnant to keep a boy or even believing that he loves you at fifteen you are sadly mistaken. It will backfire in your face or you'll realize soon after you were not ready for this whole experience, and you cannot take it back. When I found out initially I was pregnant. I was out-done and ashamed of myself! My advice to all you beautiful young ladies is DO NOT, I REPEAT, DO NOT have sex when you are not physically and mentally ready for this!!! KNOW YOUR WORTH! I want you to know you are fearfully and wonderfully made. You do not have to let it all hang out to get a boy to notice you. Your beauty comes from within. If you lose your self-respect, it is not worth it.

Kids Can Be So Cruel

I can remember one time in grade school, the other kids giving me nicknames that really were about my weight at the time that were not such nice names and I would kind of laugh it off but on the inside, I was broken. Kids were so cruel and thoughtless. They would spread rumors about without any regard for your feelings. I just never got that! It never made any sense. I thought I was broken beyond repair. I got teased quite a bit. I don't know if you could put yourself in my place or not to know what it felt like being the ampler, curvier one. I was always self-conscious. Do you know how hard it is to live up to your own expectations while other people are so busy putting you down when you're still not strong enough to fight yet? They are putting you down at every turn. Even when they pay you a compliment, you don't even know how to receive it, to the point when you're not sure they are being truthful with you or not. I was always trying to make everyone else happy around me. It didn't matter if I was happy; maybe doing that would take the focus away from me. I wouldn't have to deal with me. There were so many layers I had to peel back to heal. I know I was still in there somewhere. I knew deep down inside I was a diamond but I was stuck in the rough.

My high school days were not happy ones, for the most part. I was always trying to find my niche! Puberty is no joke. You go through growth spurts. You start getting breasts and your body gets curvier. You get your menstrual cycle and that means you can get pregnant, and if that isn't enough pubic hair and armpit hair and acne. Oh, my goodness, then on top of all that, trying not to be curious about sex! You have got to be kidding, biggest trick ever!

When I was in school if you got in trouble and went to the principal's office you would get paddled with the paddle with the holes in it. That was no joke, kids know nothing about that nowadays. When you got bad grades, you were put on punishment until the next quarter grades came out, you couldn't go outside and play or

The Emotional Fire

watch TV or talk on the phone with your friends. You had to stay on your punishment too!! There was no getting out of it till it was over. Parents can hardly take electronic gadgets from their kids these days without them acting like they can't do without them. Wonder what would happen if they went back to talking to each other! What a concept HA! HA! I remember how much fun it was to play outside but you had to get your butt in the house before the street light went out or you would get your butt dusted!! I think we all have our childhood memories, some fond and not so fond ones.

I sometimes felt so crushed and defeated and so alone, but I had to continue to move on even when I felt like giving up. I would say to myself *what would my girls think about their mom if she just gave up and did not fight for her family?* I did not want them to be disappointed in me ever! I thought by keeping them shielded from some things, I was being a mom and protecting my babies. All the things I was going through in every phase of my life were part of a journey of life's lessons. I had to push on even though I would feel like I could not go on any further. I tried to keep my head up and work as hard as I could to make ends meet and keep it together.

I guess you're wondering by now why not go to my parents for help. I felt like I had to be responsible for my own actions and decisions I made in my life. It was my bed and I had to lie in it. I know they would have been there for me if I needed them any time! In my head these were the choices I made so I had to work them out on

Cynthia Powell

my own to the best of my ability. I always felt like I was in a raging inferno. I would have to make each choice and would hope I was making the right ones and could put that fire out! Who does not want to live an amazing life? I wanted to give my girls the best life as well! I may not have gotten the breaks that other people did nor have known the right people to get me where I needed to be. I tried to do my best with what I could on my own merit. The things I was hearing that other people were doing to get jobs back then, I definitely was not stooping that low. I needed a good paying job with some good insurance for the girls and I thought I finally found a good one at the nursing home as a C.N.A., once I got in you could sign up to work extra hours because the call-in rate was high. You could work plenty of hours but they were long and hard ones.

The insurance benefits sucked but I had to do what I had to do until I could do better. The nursing home was short-staffed all the time. Employees would call off quite a lot. It could be a bit much at times but I was grateful I had job. I was still searching for the right one going through the process to get to my best. I eventually ended up working three jobs for ten years before I could slow down. It was a struggle, I did not know if I was coming or going, but I know I had to keep on pushing to survive. I was still searching for my dream job. I was looking for that bright light at the end of the tunnel. It could be so frustrating!!

Let me say this, you can come across your dream job but you can encounter people that

The Emotional Fire

make your work life miserable. At that time, I could not understand why people kept up so much confusion in the workplace. Some of the other employees would talk about people behind their backs and try to set them up to fail. When you are not like that at all it can be a hard pill to swallow. I still want to believe that there are some genuine people in the world and everyone is not trying to hurt you all time! I would meet new people at the job. I still was not totally trusting because of my past experiences. It seemed every time I would try to trust people they would do things to purposely hurt me. I did not bother anyone, I just came to work, did my work and went home when the day was done.

    I went through some mind-boggling things like I would walk up on people talking about me. I did not deserve this by any means. I do not care how much money you make, there is always some crap to deal with. I had one of my co-workers walk up to me one day to tell me that somebody I had befriended was talking about me. They then proceeded to call that person so I could hear that person talking about me. I wonder how you'd feel if that happened to you? Maybe you could get some idea of just how I felt! I had more respect for that person who let me know the real deal than somebody who pretended they cared about me! I knew at least where I stood with them as opposed to putting my life in the hands of that two-faced person. It truly was a worrisome and bumpy ride. I still pushed forward trying to make my life better and try to get it on track within my means. I had no idea what direction I was going, whether I was at a standstill or moving forward.

I just kept pushing. I was always filling out applications, hoping I could get some relief from worrying about having some decent insurance and being able to make it! There is no fun in living from paycheck to paycheck. Despite all the adversity, I was going through. My girls we're growing up before my eyes and I just wanted them to stay innocent babies forever so no one could hurt or mistreat them in any way. I couldn't help it! I was just being a mom.

Girls really need their mom just like boys really need their dad! I did the best I could to raise them well, but I felt I did not do nearly enough. I was going through some emotional things myself which would cause me to not be as attentive to their needs at times. I would try to make it fun for them when we did spend quality time together. I loved the time we spent together.

I don't think children understand how you feel as a parent when they start wanting to hang out with their friends and spend less time with you. It would make me feel left out. When they would leave to go with their friends I would cry because I knew they were growing up. I could not protect them like I could when they were little. It just bothered me to let go and release them out into this world. It could be a very cruel and complicated place at times! I did not want them to go through anything at all. I just wished they could be my babies forever!

The Emotional Fire

I must tell you my voyage as a young mother was not an easy one considering the fact that I was fifteen years old at the time. I was still trying to figure my own self out past puberty into a young adult. The fire of emotions consumed me. I had to try to be a mature girl because I was someone's mother now! For goodness sake, I was fifteen!

CHAPTER 6

This Struggle Was Real

What did I know about being somebody's mom at my age! I had to struggle with it at the beginning, but I tried the best I could. I carried this mental conflict into adulthood. I realized in hindsight there was something I still had not come to grips with yet. It added internal fuel to the fire of emotions that stirred inside of me. I still did not understand the firestorm of emotion at all! What should I do?

Keeping in mind as I have said before at that time in my life I was not talking to anyone because of the things I'd been through, I did not talk much as a young person either. It was the same when it came to the most awful thing that happened to me ever!!! I was molested at the age of ten. I did not tell my parents about this at all. How do you begin to tell your parents, at ten? I had no concept of it mentally or physically at all!!! I did not know where to begin to tell them this happened to me. I was dazed and confused. For goodness sake, my mentality at that age! I thought I did something to cause it, but I know that wasn't true. I sure did not know how to even

The Emotional Fire

start saying it! It happened to me more than once. One person I didn't know the other one I knew well but, at the age that I was, I did not know how to process any of it! I felt so lost and destroyed and empty! It was something bad that happened to me on my life's journey but it does not define who I am! It happened to me over a period of time. I was not in a good headspace during this time at all! I tried my best not to let it affect me or my life. It was not easy. I did not encourage this nor did I deserve this at all. I was ten for God's sake!!! I was still playing with dolls. I was innocent. I did not have a clue. I was totally traumatized! I tried my best to forget about it every day. I was acting out in my own way. I was sitting in my room in the dark on a regular basis. I tried to get it out of my head! As the weeks went by I decided I would try to bury it down deep. At times, I would think to myself I would be better off no longer being in this world. God was ordering my steps even then! If I tell you I had a handle on it, I did not. It was a crazy, emotional ride at that age. I cannot imagine even younger children than I went through this.

In each of us that have been through some trauma in our life there is a young suffering child that needs to be healed! To protect ourselves against any future pain we often try to forget what happened to us. I realize every time we have some pain in our life, we think we can handle it. We bury it deep down inside our unconscious mind. It might be that we are afraid to face this child for years to come. Just because we ignore this inner child does not mean he/she is not there.

Cynthia Powell

The hurt child is always around, calling out to us to get our attention to let us know they're here. That we cannot avoid, no matter how much we try. We try to end our suffering by burying that inner child deep inside and staying as far away as possible. I realized that at some point trying to run from it does not end the pain. It only prolongs it. My wounded child is lying inside of me. I really needed some guidance on how to begin to love and heal my inner child.

As I was maturing, I always felt like I was not good enough. It was much deeper than me. I would become withdrawn and my self-esteem was not good at all. I felt powerless and out of control. I headed into puberty with promiscuity issues. It would also make me understand my using food to mask my pain. The emotional and physical distress of being sexually molested can destroy you if you let it.

I never talked to anyone about being molested. I carried it into adulthood. I remember the day it came back to me. It happened about three years ago. I was watching a program one day and they had a segment on young children being molested, and it triggered that memory and the tears just started flowing. The incident came back like a raging inferno with no way to put out this fire. I felt emotionally numb. I felt sick! I felt disgusted with myself! I felt so alone! All the feelings you could of possibly imagine, I went through them. It felt like I was floating outside of my body for sure! I have been trying to work through and sort out my feelings one at a time since then. I did not know who to talk to at this point. I guess I was in

The Emotional Fire

denial and trying to forget and erase it from my mind. Sometimes people who are close to you think they are ready to hear your story but they're not! I felt so violated and I trusted no one with what happened for fear they would say I caused it and it was entirely my fault! What could I have done at ten for someone to feel like they could just devastate me like that! My innocence was taken from me. I never thought and felt the same again!!!!

At that time after the molestation happened to me I was walking around wondering if anyone could tell. I was not sleeping well and I was having flashbacks from time to time. I felt so dirty, guilty and embarrassed. I went through fear; anger and rage, loss of control and feeling powerless. I had changes in sexuality and intimacy. I also had physical symptoms and self-blame issues and low self-esteem. I was a wreck on the inside! On top of that I started my menstrual cycle at an early age! I am trying to wrap my head around that whole situation It turned my young world upside down! My head was not even on thinking about boys or anything like that at all! I walked around every day at the beginning of my pre-teen life wondering if I was good enough. I wondered if I was even worth loving because of what happened to me. If that was a possibility in my distant future I was in a daze all the time. I suppressed all my feelings. I did not want to talk at all. I just felt hopeless! I felt emotional but I was trying to put on a happy face on the outside. I had to face the reality that the past abuse was a process. It felt like I was frozen in ice--seen but out of reach. To open my heart to this truth was devastating. Even though I did not know where I should start, I felt a meltdown would be a disaster. I was searing full of emotions but I must reflect on my grade school into high school chapter of my life. It was a struggle for me because I was always trying to get in where I could fit in! It was not the right fit and I would end up with the bad kids as they would be labeled but you know they would accept me and treat me better than some of my so-called good friends at times. They would do some mischievous things and I would be right there with them even though I know I would get my butt in trouble for hanging with them! All this off-kilter behavior wasn't good for me at all!

How Do I Heal

When or how do I start to heal? Where do I begin? Will, I ever feel worthy or good enough? I wish I knew what to do to get me on the right track to start my healing journey!! There is nothing like another human being making you feel like you're useless when at that moment, you don't begin to have the strength to fight back yet! Even though I had all these thoughts and concerns going through my head, I still had to keep on pushing forward because life goes on. It does not just stop and let you get off! I had to understand that there is no end to healing and there are going to be good days, bad days but my hope was that the hard days would become less and less. I had to do something to release my heart and soul. I decided to write an open letter

The Emotional Fire

to my abuser to help me heal and maybe it will also heal someone's soul to read this as well:

Open letter to the person who stole my innocence from me! In a million years, I never would have thought I would be a part of number of young women who had to put up with abuse in their lifetime. During the time it happened to me, I never imagined the changes it would take me through in my life. Whenever I heard about someone who had been through this same kind of pain It really touched my heart in a way of deep sadness. Even if I have ran into you off and on at some point in my life. I act like I did not see you and I did not acknowledge what you did to me. I saw that you were having problems in your own life from the consequences of your actions. I had to try to save myself and start working on loving me.

I wrote this to help face any demons I have been holding onto for so long. That one thought that made me think it was my fault. I want to face this pain head on and write all that is hidden in my heart. To hug and hold that inner child and tell her everything is going to be alright! To the person who had no reason or right to hurt me. By forcing yourself on me and I had to

Cynthia Powell

fight with every ounce of strength I had in me. I was so afraid I didn't know what to do. I was ten for God's sake. I was an innocent child and you were much older than me. I felt like shit and I felt so violated. I thought I was ugly and damaged goods. You have no idea you change my life forever. I never looked at things the same again. I feared trusting anyone who told me they love me and my image of myself felt like it had been trampled on. I blamed myself for it happening. I thought if you could go through this same thing you took me through. I knew I could never wish that on any of your family member. How can your ass sleep at night after what you did to me? I held on to this pain all these years and I couldn't forgive myself for trusting you. But I realized I had to try to let it go and finally forgive myself. I had to stop reliving it over again. I had to stop blaming myself because it wasn't my fault. I had to let go to free my soul and I had to forgive for me to move on. I had to hope that one day when I was ready I would meet someone who would love me for who I am. He would look through the hurt and pain and see my beautiful soul and never hurt me like you did. I had to hold on to the thought that my creator was keeping me strong. I don't know if you ever felt bad for what you did to me or if you hurt anyone else the way you did me. My prayer is that one day when you reflect on this in your mind and get some sense about yourself. I am so glad I never saw your face again to remind me of the hurt you inflicted on me. I did that enough to myself over the years. You took my innocence from me that I could never get back.

P.S. You may never get to read this. I am trying my best to take what happened to me and try to turn it into a positive and make better choices in my life. My hope is by talking about this it will give a voice to others who have lost theirs, and let them know to keep their head up and there is hope for life after abuse. I pray peace, love and blessing to each soul in pain. I send healing blessing to you all.

Rollercoaster Ride

Heading into my pre-teens it was truly a rollercoaster ride of emotions. While I thought I was handling what happened to me. I was really acting out. I was sad and then happy and I would cry. I would also isolate myself. I would second guess myself. I would beat myself up. OH, MY GOODNESS I went through all stages of horrendous emotions. Every aspect of my life I encountered I would have to talk myself through it. I would think was I doing the right thing or not. I did not want to talk to anyone about anything I had a question about because I would be horrified that they would say I was stupid or I did not know what I was doing. This dismal event would touch every facet of my life. I really tried the best I knew how to work through it.

The ninth through twelve grades were a flaming and vivid trail of emotional events in my life that at times I had no full understanding of! I became someone's mom even when I had no sense of my own self. I was still in self-discovery mode. I would go to school dances and join school clubs hoping somehow, I could find a way to fit in. I was still not sure of the relationship thing. I was not even sure who I was!

Leonardo had taken me through so many emotions all the time we were together I did not know the real me or who that really was! How do you explain how or what you're feeling, when you do not even know? I just know that I tried to treat him like I wanted to be treated, even though I did not get that in return at times. I had to try to figure out a way to believe in and love myself. I had to take a chance even if it was hard. Even when it did not make sense to me during that time, I had to fake it until it changed. I had to try to work through the dark parts of myself. I would to peel back one layer at a time to find the real me. It was not an easy task. Sometimes while peeling back the layers I would get stuck and not know which direction I should go in! All these things affected every part of my life. I was in such a dark place at times that I felt like even

The Emotional Fire

God could not hear me. I felt so trapped and helpless at times. I tried to stay hopeful that I would have the power and strength to come out on the other side, in a place of serenity that was my hope. I remember times I couldn't get out the bed or even get dressed--it truly was an inner fire that needed to be put out! I tried my best to go on with my life. I had to still take care of my kids and work and function as much as possible. I still wanted to do things to better myself my children as well as myself. I continued to look for a better job. I would try just to immerse myself in looking for a better job, hoping that would take my attention temporarily.

Just when I thought all hope was lost, I heard from the one job that I had my sights on. I had been calling and checking on my application so much, until they knew me on a first-name basis! I finally got an interview. I was so excited! Little did I know it was only a first interview? I would have to come back two more times over a period of two months before I finally got hired! I was elated. This was the job I could retire from! My first day hired as a janitor at this facility was interesting.

CHAPTER 7

This Facility Was Interesting

The buildings were so huge the site itself was amazing to see at first glance! There was so much to see! The day I started, they put me with someone to show me the ropes. I was very fortunate to have a nice and patient person to help me through this process. My boss at that time told me I would have this help for a week then I would be on my own, needless to say that help lasted for three days and they put me on my own. I guess it did not matter if it was three days or week either, I would sink or swim I suppose! I made it through the work initiation, so to speak!

As time went on I really enjoyed working there. I met some nice co-workers, so it made coming to work enjoyable. It was about time to be able to work somewhere and love coming to it too! The site was so big you could take beautiful nature walks and see the most wonderful views. I thought it was the best place ever to be employed at. What place could you work at and like being there every day? They also had different monthly activities you could attend. The first few years it was an amazing place to work. There were always events going on you

The Emotional Fire

could attend! What more could you ask for than enjoy working and having things to do as well! I finally felt like things were looking up. I was so excited there was even a chance in the future to advance to better jobs! I thought that was a beautiful thing!!!

I was so used to it being such a nice place to work at so when things started to change over time it was hard to grasp. The co-workers I worked with were just like family members we were close! We would work together as a unit to get things done! When it started changing it totally busted my bubble!! As time went on and they hired a new set of people to work in our custodial group, it was not the same. The new people were a different breed, instead of just doing the work in the building together to make us all look good they just turned into a bunch of tattle-tales and troublemakers. The building administrator just wanted us to keep the building up and when he needed something done that we were on top of it. People know they could be something else at times! There was always one that had a mind of their own and didn't want to cooperate with everyone else to get the job done!

Now keep in mind I still had personal baggage I needed to release and sort out which means I let my guard down and sometimes things didn't work out like I wanted them to. As a matter of fact, it was a crappy deal at times. I never understood who or what started this bonfire. It really was quite petty!! One thing I did learn is when you try to explain to someone what you're going through with that person and because they are not experiencing that same thing, their perception of that is they just don't get it!! It can be quite frustrating! I would say the lab was a very wonderful place for me for about three years! After that I started to notice a few changes. I must tell you though, I did get to meet some very interesting and nice people as well as some butt holes! The foreman would put you with a partner to get work done. I don't know if this was a good practice or not because if your partner didn't like you, they would report to the boss that they did all the work when they really did not! It was also funny how the boss would just believe what the other person said because they had worked there longer! How people have a perception of you off the way you look that always amazed me!

I realized just how naïve I was to think for the most part people were kind but after being here a few years it taught me a lot of life lessons! Some of the lessons I wasn't ready for at all especially the backstabbing and the backbiting! I still enjoyed working there and I learned so much about floor care and extracting carpet. I can honestly say that I really liked going to the job. It wasn't the job, it was the people. There is good and bad people everywhere you go. What is hard is they don't show themselves right away. They are like a thief in the night. They come to bring your destruction and downfall! This is what they come to work for to make other people's lives miserable because they are miserable! That is so sad! I realized I was starting to work with some co-workers that didn't like me. They didn't even know me. I

The Emotional Fire

thought I was done going through this high school stuff. Little did I know the adults were worse? I thought I was done going through this crap! I am still in fiery turmoil myself but I had to try to keep moving forward even if I had not put out all the fires in my life. I realized the lab was its own world for sure. I understood early on I had to learn to live in my own uniqueness. It was a process, no doubt about it. It wasn't easy at all. I had an incident where the foreman would put you with a partner so we could work together but when we would get back to check in, that other person would say they did all the work but it was the other way around. I realized people were still talking about me. How could somebody talk about if you were lazy or did any work or not if they have never worked with you? People are so special at times they just go off gossip.

I was still going through my weight challenges but that didn't mean I was lazy, but some people would try to make it seem that way! I must say working at the faculty overtime was a horse of another color, a city of its own so to speak. It was an experience to learn from it. It could either make you or break you. I realized just how much I didn't know until I stepped into that world! What a way to break you in for the real world outside the faculty Ha! Ha! How does that saying go when life gives you lemons make lemonade, or the other special one, it is what it is!

I would still have to say that being molested at a young age touched every aspect of my life, it affected how I interacted with people and whether I would speak up for myself! I would alienate myself from people as well! It bothered me that I would not speak up for myself when something would go down. I would get triggers at times that would cause me intensely emotional responses at times that I didn't even understand. It made me feel powerless, vulnerable, shameful and full of guilt sometimes.

If they said I did it, I would just take the blame! It was bitter pill for me swallow. It made me feel so powerless and incapable of accomplishing anything at all! It influenced my relationships with my friends because at times I felt like I had to do certain things to fit in so I would be accepted. It was so crazy because a lot of these things were not what I was about at all! I knew this was something I struggled with at that time and I just did not know what to do! I would go the extra mile and overcompensate. You know I would still get blamed for stuff I did not do! I always felt that I had to explain everything, even when it did not call for it.

It also affected my relationships with guys. I would sometime confuse sex with love after experiencing physical and mental abuse with being powerless or in some instances powerful! I would also at times get triggers like places and the way I was touched, smells, sounds, feelings I experienced! I didn't know how to talk to my partner about what I went through because I did not want them to look at me any differently, it was hard enough for me already. I had problems with intimacy! It was so annoying still trying to find myself. I had to realize something about myself at that time whether I wanted to face it or

The Emotional Fire

not I was not very confident, I didn't like myself very much and I tried to hide it the best I could to the best of my ability. I did not let people see the real me and how much they were hurting me and trying to crush my spirit!! I tried to turn as much of it as I could into a positive reinforcement! Some days I succeeded better than others. At times it was a fiery force to be reckoned with!

I would hang out with my good girlfriends sometimes. I loved them very much we were more like sisters than girlfriends really! But hanging out with them at the club was always interesting for certain, the guys were more attracted to them than me. I became the designated purse and drink watcher. This became a long-standing joke of mine. Hence, I was not always excited about hanging out with the girls because I was always odd women out. At that time to society fat was not where it's at for sure! As time went on Big Beautiful Women have come a long way. In this world if you're not big enough to hula hoop through a Cheerio they will consider you being overweight! It can make you feel self-conscious. I still tried to overcome it. When someone would pay me a compliment I would think in my head they were just trying to be nice and they didn't mean it. I was always in my feelings and my defenses were always up. Most situations I felt like a third wheel but I still tried to get out of the house anyway!!! It could be a very lonely place. I still tried to keep my head held high no matter what or how I was feeling! Working on my best self I knew this would be a special undertaking. So, I wouldn't feel so overwhelmed I would tell myself 'Baby steps, everything is going to be fine!' I had to change how I felt so it could help change my thoughts from negative to a positive. I must learn how to feel good about me. I had to start believing in myself more and understand I had good qualities and love me more and learn not to beat myself up so. There will be times in your life that you make mistakes along the way but it isn't the end of the world! I had to get back to what I knew--my faith and trust in God--to help me get back to where I needed to be. It would confuse me at times, though, how people could kick you when you're down and hoping you would stay there. What a concept it would be if people could be considerate of each other's feelings. If they would put themselves in other people's shoes and thought about how they felt. What an amazing world this would be! I had to learn to become my own cheerleader and keep myself lifted as much as I could within my means.

I had to start somewhere back on this journey of how to love me again. I had to remember the person that did this to me was the only one to blame. Also, the negative feelings I had acquired came from the fact of what happened to me. I had to start to learn how to deal with the flashbacks and unpleasant memories, and begin to reconnect to my body and my feelings. Since I didn't really have anyone I could trust to talk to about this, I had to try to help my own self the best way I knew how. I had to somehow tap in to my inner strength. I had to get back to interact with people and try to trust again if that was possible, and not let it

The Emotional Fire

devastate me even if I got let down. I had to do all I could to move on with my life. I was determined to do so, no matter what! It was like you were on a road trip, you never knew where you were going and what you would encounter. I couldn't give up on me!

I had to start to work on healing my inside and my self-esteem. I had to get a better opinion of myself and just start loving on me. Maybe by loving on me I will stop beating myself up or dragging me down over simple mistakes. I was willing to give it a try. I was going to stop being my worst enemy too. Who can beat up on themselves better than anyone? We can do it to ourselves the best. Another good place for me to start was by learning how to handle and replace that voice of the inner critic. That inner voice can either whispers or shouts negativity in your head. I had to learn to ignore it and not to accept all that stuff. I had to just keep my thoughts on the constructive tip. Even when someone would try to beat up on me emotionally, I would have to remember my strengths so I could answer back. I had to remember my strengths, especially at my lowest so I had to have some daily reminders to keep me in the right head space. I had to come up with some affirmations for myself. I realized self-blame was a real thing. You just blame yourself for everything, whether it is your fault or not. You find blaming yourself for being overweight and unskilled. You even blame yourself for how people react to you, apologizing for things you didn't even cause so you must keep yourself encouraged. It was a constant battle.

Cynthia Powell

I had to also take out the time to appreciate me to keep on that positive road. When you're used to that negative place, it is really a true journey. I had to understand I was not perfect and I could try to be my best self. When I make mistakes, I just handle them in the most positive way. I must be my own best friend. I couldn't compare myself to others and what they have because I could never achieve the things I want in this life by doing that. So, I was really trying to put my best foot forward. I wanted to start being around more positive, uplifting people, true human beings that are kind and loving. I want to believe that they do exist.

Forgiving yourself is not an easy task but you must be able to do it so you can move on with your life. You can walk around being broken and hurt. Understand making the choice to move on and heal is long, hard and very hurtful at times, letting go of the past that was full of pain takes time. It takes a lot of work. Even though the ride can be rough as hell, you have to believe it is worth going through to find some peace. I know it can be difficult sometimes to forgive people who hurt you deeply because it opens old wounds. It forces you to relive the pain all over again and admit how shitty you felt in the first place. It may bring about some resentment that blocks you from dealing with the pain. You may even think if forgiving the people who hurt you will bring up some scary emotions and some mind-blowing questions. You know if you don't work on forgiveness it will cause you to hold grudges, hold on to resentment, and hold on to your pain of the past.

The Emotional Fire

Just because you forgive the people who hurt you doesn't mean you erase that painful or trauma from your mind. Nothing we could do thus far has been able to turn back the hands of time and remove all the pain and anguish from our life journey and forgiving won't do that. You can't forget, nor should you. The painful things that happened to you can teach you so much about not being pushed around again or doing the same to someone else. We must be honest with ourselves that we may not be ready to forgive, and that is okay, instead of pretending to forgive. I also had to learn to love and accept myself and that had to come from the inside. I had to understand I didn't have to be different to be worthy. My true self was the center of love and inner goodness. I was a beautiful soul. I might have buried my inner light, but it wasn't possible to destroy it. Loving yourself is an ongoing thing. I had to begin by appreciating me. I had to get up reminding myself of my worth. I would have to use some affirmations to stay positive. I had to learn to be patient with myself. Also, to love the good and the not so good things. about me. Remember just because healing has taken place that doesn't mean the damage never happened. It just means that this damage doesn't have to take control of your life. Never be ashamed of your journey you have been on to get you where you need to be, because it will help to inspire others. No matter what has happened in your life, know you have the strength. You can't change what happened physically and emotionally, but you have the power to come back from it. Your past has no power over your present. You are so much stronger than you give yourself credit for! In my situation overcoming meant to be able to not let the abuse that happened in my past define me. It's something that happened to me but it is not who I am. You will either walk through your journey and face it or be on the outside looking in and struggling to KNOW YOUR WORTH! Which one will you choose? Remember it is about you and your life's journey. CHOOSE YOU!!!

As I continue my journey of self-improvement I hope these words will help you on your voyage to making you feel whole again and remember you are fearfully and wonderfully made! I used to let other people put me down, I use to think I was disposable, easy to ignore and trivial, and didn't deserve anyone's respect—not even my own. I no longer use food to handle my feelings. I know now that I matter!!!

Never forget were you've come from, and everything you have made it through. All the time you pushed yourself even when you felt like you couldn't. All those mornings you got out of the bed no matter how hard that was. All the times you wanted to throw in the towel but you managed to make it through another day. Know that you can make it and there are better days ahead!!! Know that the fire does not have to continue to burn or smolder. It can be extinguished!

The Emotional Fire

Remember, Your Current Situation Does Not Define Your Destiny!

I leave you with my Healing Letter. As I am on my healing journey, and you are my focus. I thought that food would make me feel better, when I was pain because I did not have to explain myself to it or even worry about it. I would just let people talk about me and not speak up for myself. I felt like no one saw me. I felt like I was easy to ignore, to trivial to be called to mind, and I did not deserve anyone's admiration including my own. I tried to act like nothing ever bothered me and hopefully nobody would notice how inadequate I was feeling! I do not try to measure up with other people any longer. I know longer use food for comfort. I understand know that I matter and I do have something to offer.

I am doing well, and I plan on doing even more amazing! I might visit every now and then, I have no intention on every going back to that painful place I have been before. I plan to move forward away from darkness into the marvelous light. I want to leave all the hurt and insecurities and awful pain behind me, without forgetting what happened and the lessons I learned from it. I know there is a place for me in this world. I will move forward in positivity. I send you love and encouragement no matter where you are on your road to healing! Remember you are the master of your own destiny! You can influence and control your environment! You can make your life whatever you want it to be!

Glossary of Terms

Alienated Cause (someone) to feel isolated or estranged

Anorexia A lack or loss of appetite for food (as a medical condition).

Apprehensive Anxious or fearful that something bad or unpleasant will happen.

Binge A short period devoted to indulging in an activity to excess, especially drinking alcohol or eating.

Bulimia An emotional disorder involving distortion of body image and an obsessive desire to lose weight.

Bulimia An eating disorder in which a large quantity of food is consumed in a short period, often followed by feelings of guilt or shame.

Catastrophe An event causing great and often sudden damage or suffering a disaster.

The Emotional Fire

Compulsive   Resulting from or relating to an irresistible urge, especially one that is against one's conscious wishes.

Critical   Expressing adverse or disapproving comments or judgments.

Denial   The action of declaring something to be untrue.

Destiny   The events that will necessarily happen to a person or thing in the future.

Devastated   Destroy or ruin (something)

Disregard   Pay no attention to; ignore.

Distracted   Unable to concentrate because one's mind is pre-occupied.

Hormones   A person's sex hormones as held to influence behavior or mood.

Immature   Not fully developed.

Initiation   The action of admitting someone into a secret or obscure society or group, typically, with a ritual.

Intense   Of extreme force, degree or strength

Melanin	A dark brown to black pigment occurring in hair, skin, and iris of the eye in people and animals.
Merit	The quality of being particularly good or worthy, especially so as to deserve praise or reward.
Notion	A conception of belief about something.
Oppression	To persecute or subjugate by force.
Optimistic	Hopeful and confident about the future.
Puberty	The period during which adolescents reach sexual maturity and become capable of reproduction.
Rage	Violent, uncontrollable anger.
Recovery	A return to a normal state of health, mind, or strength.
Self-conscious	Feeling undue awareness of oneself, one's appearance, or one's action.
Traumatic	Emotionally disturbing or distressing

The Emotional Fire

Typical Having the distinctive qualities of a particular type of person or thing.

Vulnerable Susceptible to physical or emotional attack or harm.

www.ingramcontent.com/pod-product-compliance
Lightning Source LLC
Chambersburg PA
CBHW071159090426
42736CB00012B/2380